Embark on a Transformative Coding Journey with:

"Coding with Python: From First Steps to Advanced Mastery"

Table of Contents

We are adding a bonus tutorial on HTML and CSS, especially considering how often these technologies are used alongside Python in web development.

1. Introduction to Web Development
2. Getting Started with HTML
3. Diving Deeper into HTML
4. Introduction to CSS
5. Advanced CSS Techniques
6. Integrating HTML and CSS
7. Next Steps in Web Development

Dive into the world of Python programming with this

comprehensive guide, perfect for beginners and seasoned coders alike. "Coding with Python: From First Steps to Advanced Mastery" is a must-have e-book for anyone looking to enhance their programming skills and grasp the full potential of Python.

Why Choose This Python Programming Book?

Beginner-Friendly Approach: Start with the basics of Python and gradually progress to more complex concepts.

Hands-On Learning: Engage with practical examples, real-world projects, and interactive exercises.

Comprehensive Coverage: From fundamental syntax to advanced features like web development, data science, and machine learning.

Python Best Practices: Learn to write clean, efficient, and Pythonic code.

What's Inside?

Fundamental Python Concepts: Understand variables, data types, and basic operations.

Advanced Python Features: Delve into list comprehensions, generators, decorators, and context managers.

Real-World Applications: Build web applications using Flask and Django and explore data science tools like NumPy and Pandas.

Machine Learning Basics: Get a primer on using Python for AI and machine learning projects.

Project-Based Learning: Solidify your knowledge by building a practical Python application.

For Whom Is This Book?

Aspiring Programmers: Kickstart your programming journey

with Python.

Coding Enthusiasts: Expand your existing programming knowledge to Python.

Career Advancers: Add Python to your skillset for professional growth in tech, data science, and more.

Your Path to Python Mastery Starts Here

"Packed with expert insights, clear explanations, and real-world examples, 'Coding with Python: From First Steps to Advanced Mastery' is your roadmap to becoming proficient in one of the most versatile programming languages of our time. Whether you're aiming to break into the tech industry, or simply looking to add a valuable skill to your repertoire, this e-book is your ideal companion."

We are adding a <u>bonus tutorial</u> on HTML and CSS, especially considering how often these technologies are used alongside Python in web development.

"Master Web Development with Our Comprehensive HTML and CSS Tutorial: Dive into our insightful bonus tutorial on HTML and CSS, designed for both beginners and intermediate web developers. This essential guide covers everything from building basic web page layouts to advanced techniques for integrating HTML and CSS. Enhance your skills with best practices for structuring your code, ensuring cross-browser compatibility, and effective debugging methods. Progress to dynamic web page creation with an introduction to JavaScript and explore modern web development frameworks. Equip yourself with the knowledge and practical skills to excel in the ever-evolving world of web development. Perfect for aspiring web designers and developers, this tutorial is your stepping-stone to mastering web development."

Unlock your coding potential – Download your copy today and take the first step towards mastering Python!

CHAPTER 1: INTRODUCTION TO PYTHON

Welcome to the World of Python!

Imagine you're a wizard, and in your hands, you hold a wand that can create almost anything in the digital world. This wand is Python, one of the most popular and powerful programming languages in the world today. Python is like a magic wand for developers, a tool that helps bring ideas to life in the form of websites, games, scientific research, and much more.

Each chapter will include practical examples, exercises for the reader, and a summary of key points to reinforce learning. This structure is designed to progressively build the reader's Python skills, from basic concepts to more advanced applications, ensuring a thorough understanding of the language.

WHY PYTHON?

Python is renowned for its simplicity and readability, making it a favorite among beginners and experts alike. It's like learning the English of the programming world – straightforward, yet incredibly powerful. Here's why Python is so loved:

Easy to Learn: Python's syntax is clean and simple, which makes it easy to learn. It's like writing instructions in plain English, but these instructions make computers do amazing things.

Versatile: From building websites to analyzing data, Python can do it all. It's like a Swiss Army knife for programming.

Strong Community: With millions of Pythonistas (Python enthusiasts) around the globe, you'll never walk alone on your coding journey. There's always someone to help, share, and collaborate with.

Career Opportunities: Knowing Python opens doors in many industries. Whether it's web development, data science, artificial intelligence, or scientific computing, Python skills are in high demand.

Python in Action: Where is it Used?

Python isn't just about writing code, it's about creating solutions, and it's being used in some really cool ways:

Web Development: Websites like Reddit, Pinterest, and Instagram are built with Python. It helps in handling databases, server-side operations, and even designing the look and feel of a website.

Data Science and Machine Learning: Python sorts, analyzes, and visualizes data. It's a key tool in making sense of large datasets and building AI models that predict, learn, and make smart decisions.

Automation: Got boring, repetitive tasks? Python can automate them for you. From organizing files to sending emails, Python can be your personal assistant.

Scientific and Numeric Computing: Scientists use Python for complex calculations and simulations, making breakthroughs in their fields.

Game Development: Python adds logic and functionality in games. It's behind the scenes, making the gaming world more interactive and fun.

Conclusion

As you embark on this journey, remember that learning Python is like learning to play an instrument. It takes practice, patience, and a lot of fun along the way. Each line of code you write is a note, and with each program, you compose a symphony. So, grab your wand, and let's start casting some Python spells!

This introduction sets the stage for an engaging and informative journey into Python programming. Each chapter following this would delve deeper into Python's syntax, its libraries, and how to create real-world projects. Whether the reader is a total beginner or looking to expand their programming knowledge, this book would be a guide to understanding and loving Python.

CHAPTER 2: FIRST STEPS WITH PYTHON

Embarking on Your Python Adventure

Welcome to the beginning of your Python journey! In this chapter, we'll walk through the initial steps of setting up Python on your computer, creating a comfortable workspace for your coding adventures, and writing your very first Python script. Let's dive in!

Installing Python

Step 1: Downloading Python

Visit the Python Website: Go to python.org, the official site for Python.

Choose Your Version: Python releases new versions regularly. As a beginner, it's best to download the latest stable version to ensure you have the most up-to-date features and security updates.

Download for Your Operating System: Python is cross-platform, meaning it works on Windows, macOS, and Linux. Select the installer that matches your operating system.

Step 2: Running the Installer

Launch the Installer: Open the downloaded file.

Select 'Install Now': On Windows, make sure to check the box that says "Add Python 3.x to PATH" before clicking 'Install Now'. This step is crucial as it allows you to run Python from the Command Prompt.

Setting Up Your Development Environment

Having the right tools and environment is key to a smooth coding experience. Here are the essentials:

Choosing a Code Editor

While you can write Python in any text editor, using a code editor designed for programming makes things much easier. Some popular choices include:

Visual Studio Code (VS Code): Versatile and feature-rich.

PyCharm: Specially designed for Python.

Sublime Text: Lightweight and fast.

Download and install the editor that appeals to you the most.

Creating Your First Python File

Open Your Code Editor: Launch the editor you installed.

Create a New File: Save it with a .py extension, for example, my_first_script.py. This tells your computer that it's a Python file.

Writing Your First Python Script

Now, let's write a simple script to see Python in action.

Type the Following Code:

python

Copy code

print("Hello, Python World!")

This line of code tells Python to display the text "Hello, Python World!" on the screen.

Save Your File: Make sure your file is saved with the changes.

Running Your Python Script

On Windows:

Open Command Prompt: You can search for it in the start menu.

Navigate to Your File: Use the cd command to change directories to where your file is saved.

Run the Script: Type python my_first_script.py and hit Enter.

On macOS and Linux:

Open Terminal: It's in your applications folder or can be found using a spotlight search.

Navigate and Run: Similar to Windows, use cd to get to your file's directory, then run it with python3 my_first_script.py.

Congratulations!

When you run your script, you should see "Hello, Python World!" printed in the command line or terminal. That's your first step into the world of Python programming! You've successfully set up your environment, written, and executed a Python script.

Key Learning Points

Python Installation: Remember to add Python to PATH during installation.

Development Environment: A good code editor can significantly enhance your coding experience.

Running Scripts: Understanding how to navigate directories and run scripts using the command line or terminal is an essential skill.

This chapter marks the very first step in your Python programming journey. As you progress, you'll learn more about the language's syntax, powerful libraries, and eventually, you'll build complex and exciting projects. But for now, take a moment to celebrate - you've just written and run your first Python program!

CHAPTER 3: PYTHON BASICS

Discovering the Building Blocks of Python

In this chapter, we'll explore the foundational elements of Python programming. Understanding variables, data types, basic operators, and how to handle input/output are crucial for your journey ahead. Let's demystify these concepts and see how they form the backbone of any Python program.

Variables: Your Data Containers

Think of variables as labeled boxes where you can store data. In Python, creating a variable is simple – you just assign a value to a name:

python

Copy code

```python
my_number = 10

my_name = "Alice"
```

Here, my_number and my_name are variables holding the values 10 and "Alice" respectively.

Dynamic Typing

Python is dynamically typed, meaning you don't need to declare the type of a variable when you create one. Python figures out the type for you:

python

Copy code

age = 30 # Python knows this is an integer

price = 19.95 # Python recognizes this as a floating-point number

is_sunny = True # Python understands this is a boolean value

Data Types: Diverse and Powerful

Data types are the classifications of the kind of data that a variable or object can hold in Python. The most common ones are:

Integers: Whole numbers without a fractional part, like 3 or -200.

Floats: Numbers with a decimal point, like 3.14 or -0.001.

Strings: Text data enclosed in quotes, like "Hello, World!".

Booleans: Represents True or False.

Basic Operators: Performing Operations on Data

Operators allow you to perform operations on variables and values. Python's basic operators include:

Arithmetic Operators:

+ Addition (e.g., 5 + 3 equals 8)

- Subtraction (e.g., 5 - 3 equals 2)

* Multiplication (e.g., 5 * 3 equals 15)

/ Division (e.g., 5 / 3 equals 1.666...)

% Modulus (e.g., 5 % 3 equals 2)

Comparison Operators:

== Equal to

!= Not equal to

> Greater than

< Less than

>= Greater than or equal to

<= Less than or equal to

Input/Output: Interacting with the User

Output with print()

The print() function is used to output data to the standard output device (like your screen):

python

Copy code

```python
print("Hello, Python!")
```

Input with input()

To get input from the user, use the input() function. It reads a line from the user and returns it as a string:

python

Copy code

```python
name = input("Enter your name: ")
print("Hello, " + name + "!")
```

Bringing It All Together: A Simple Program

Let's combine what we've learned into a small program:

python

Copy code

```python
# Ask the user for their age
age = input("Enter your age: ")
age = int(age)  # Convert the input to an integer
```

```python
# Calculate the year of birth
current_year = 2023
year_of_birth = current_year - age

# Print the result
print("You were born in the year " + str(year_of_birth) + ".")
```

This script takes the user's age as input, calculates their year of birth, and prints it out.

Key Learning Points

Variables store data and can be changed.

Data Types are important to understand as they define the kind of data you can store.

Operators let you perform calculations and comparisons.

Input/Output functions allow your program to interact with users.

Grasping these basics sets the foundation for more complex Python programming. As you progress, you'll find these concepts integral to everything you do in Python. Experiment with them, try writing small programs, and you'll find yourself becoming more comfortable and proficient in Python programming.

CHAPTER 4: FLOW CONTROL AND DECISION MAKING

Mastering the Art of Direction in Python

Welcome to the journey into the heart of Python programming - controlling the flow of your programs. In this chapter, we'll explore how to direct your program to make decisions, repeat actions, and choose its path based on certain conditions. This is where your programs start to get really interesting!

Conditional Statements: The If, Else, and Elif

Conditional statements are the backbone of decision-making in Python. They allow your program to execute certain code only when specific conditions are met.

The If Statement

The if statement is the simplest form of control structure. It checks a condition and executes a block of code if the condition is true:

python

Copy code

```python
age = 20
if age >= 18:
```

```python
    print("You are an adult.")
```

The Else and Elif Clauses

What if you want to do something else when the if condition isn't met? Enter else and elif (short for else if):

python
Copy code

```python
age = 16
if age >= 18:
    print("You are an adult.")
else:
    print("You are a minor.")
```

Use elif to check multiple conditions:

python
Copy code

```python
age = 65
if age < 18:
    print("You are a minor.")
elif age >= 65:
    print("You are a senior citizen.")
else:
    print("You are an adult.")
```

Loops: Repeating Actions

Loops are used for executing a block of code repeatedly, either a set number of times (for loops) or as long as a condition is true (while loops).

The For Loop

The for loop in Python is used to iterate over a sequence (like a list, tuple, dictionary, set, or string) and execute a block of code for each item:

python

Copy code

```python
for number in range(5):  # range(5) gives us a sequence from 0 to 4
    print(number)
```

The While Loop

A while loop will continue to execute as long as the condition is true:

python

Copy code

```python
count = 0
while count < 5:
    print(count)
    count += 1  # Increase count by 1
```

Control Statements: Break, Continue, and Pass

These statements are used to modify the behavior of loops and conditionals.

Break

break is used to exit a loop prematurely:

python

Copy code

```python
for number in range(10):
    if number == 5:
        break  # Stop the loop
    print(number)
```

Continue

continue skips the rest of the code inside a loop for the current iteration only:

python

Copy code

```python
for number in range(10):
    if number % 2 == 0:
        continue  # Skip this iteration
    print(number)  # This prints only odd numbers
```

Pass

pass is a placeholder and does nothing. It's used when a statement is required syntactically but you don't want any command or code to execute:

python

Copy code

```python
for number in range(10):
    if number % 2 == 0:
        pass  # We can decide what to do here later
    else:
        print(number)
```

A Practical Example: A Simple Menu System

Let's put these concepts into action by creating a simple menu-driven program:

python
Copy code

```python
while True:
    print("\n--- Menu ---")
    print("1. Option One")
    print("2. Option Two")
    print("3. Exit")
    choice = input("Enter your choice: ")

    if choice == "1":
        print("You chose Option One.")
    elif choice == "2":
        print("You chose Option Two.")
    elif choice == "3":
        print("Exiting the program.")
        break
    else:
        print("Invalid choice. Please try again.")
```

Key Learning Points

Conditional Statements (if, else, elif) allow your program to make decisions.

Loops (for, while) are used for repeating actions.

Control Statements (break, continue, pass) give you more control over the flow of your loops and conditionals.

Understanding these flow control mechanisms is crucial for building dynamic and responsive Python programs. As you practice, you'll find more creative and complex ways to direct your program's flow, making it smarter and more efficient. Happy coding!

CHAPTER 5: FUNCTIONS AND MODULES

Crafting and Organizing Your Python Code

Welcome to the chapter where we delve into the heart of Python's efficiency and organization - functions and modules. Understanding these concepts is crucial for writing clean, reusable, and efficient code. Let's explore how to create your own functions, use arguments and return values, and how to utilize existing modules to expand your Python capabilities.

Defining Functions

A function is a block of code that only runs when it is called. You can pass data, known as parameters, into a function. Functions help you to segment your code into logical blocks.

Creating a Basic Function

Here's how you define a simple function in Python:

python

Copy code

```python
def greet():
    print("Hello, World!")
```

To call this function, just use its name followed by parentheses:

python

Copy code

```python
greet()  # Outputs: Hello, World!
```

Function Arguments: Passing Information to Functions

Functions become more flexible and useful when they can operate on different data. This is achieved using arguments or parameters.

Example of a Function with Arguments

python

Copy code

```python
def greet(name):
    print("Hello, " + name + "!")
```

```python
greet("Alice")  # Outputs: Hello, Alice!
```

Return Values: Getting Data Out of Functions

Sometimes you want your function to process data and then send some result back. This is where return comes in.

Using Return in a Function

python

Copy code

```python
def add(a, b):
    return a + b
```

```python
result = add(5, 3)
print(result)  # Outputs: 8
```

Importing Modules: Expanding Your Toolbox

Python's real power lies in its vast collection of modules – libraries of code written by others that you can use in your own programs.

Using a Built-in Module

One of Python's built-in modules is math, which contains many useful mathematical functions.

```python
Copy code
import math

result = math.sqrt(25)
print(result)  # Outputs: 5.0
```

You can also import specific functions from a module:

```python
Copy code
from math import sqrt

result = sqrt(25)  # No need to prefix with 'math.'
print(result)  # Outputs: 5.0
```

Exploring Some Built-in Modules

Let's briefly look at a couple of commonly used built-in modules:

random: Provides functions to generate random numbers.

datetime: Supplies classes for manipulating dates and times.

The random Module

```python
Copy code
```

```python
import random

number = random.randint(1, 10)  # Generates a random integer between 1 and 10
print(number)
```

The datetime Module

python

Copy code

```python
import datetime

current_date = datetime.date.today()
print(current_date) # Outputs the current date
```

A Practical Example: A Simple Calculator

Let's create a basic calculator using functions and the math module:

python

Copy code

```python
import math

def add(a, b):
    return a + b

def subtract(a, b):
    return a - b

def multiply(a, b):
    return a * b
```

```python
def divide(a, b):
    return a / b

def square_root(a):
    return math.sqrt(a)

# Example usage
print(add(10, 5))        # 15
print(subtract(10, 5))   # 5
print(multiply(10, 5))   # 50
print(divide(10, 5))     # 2.0
print(square_root(25))   # 5.0
```

Key Learning Points

Functions are defined using the def keyword and are used to encapsulate reusable code blocks.

Arguments are used to pass data into functions.

The return statement is used to send back a value from a function.

Modules are external libraries or collections of functions and classes that you can import into your programs to extend functionality.

With a solid understanding of functions and modules, you're well on your way to writing more structured, efficient, and reusable Python code. These concepts are fundamental in any Python programmer's toolkit and will serve as a foundation for more complex programming tasks ahead. Happy coding!

CHAPTER 6: DATA STRUCTURES IN PYTHON

Organizing and Managing Data Effectively

In this chapter, we delve into the world of Python's data structures - essential tools for effectively organizing, storing, and manipulating data. Understanding lists, tuples, sets, and dictionaries will greatly enhance your ability to handle various data types in Python.

Lists: Flexible and Dynamic Arrays

A list in Python is an ordered collection of items that can be changed and updated. Lists are versatile and can hold a variety of item types.

Creating and Using Lists

python

Copy code

```python
my_list = [1, 2, 3, "Python", "Rocks"]
print(my_list)  # [1, 2, 3, 'Python', 'Rocks']
```

Accessing List Items: Use the index (starts at 0).

python

Copy code

```python
print(my_list[3]) # Python
```

Modifying Lists: Add, remove, or change items.

python

Copy code

```python
my_list.append("!")
print(my_list) # [1, 2, 3, 'Python', 'Rocks', '!']
```

Tuples: Immutable Sequences

Tuples are similar to lists, but they are immutable – you can't change their size or contents after they're created.

Creating and Using Tuples

python

Copy code

```python
my_tuple = (1, 2, 3, "Python")
print(my_tuple) # (1, 2, 3, 'Python')
```

Accessing Tuple Items: Like lists, but remember, you cannot modify tuples.

Sets: Unique and Unordered Collections

A set is an unordered collection of unique items. Sets are great for membership testing and eliminating duplicate entries.

Creating and Using Sets

python

Copy code

```python
my_set = {1, 2, 3, 3, 2}
print(my_set) # {1, 2, 3} - duplicates are removed
```

Set Operations: Union, intersection, difference, etc.

python

Copy code

```python
another_set = {3, 4, 5}
print(my_set.union(another_set))  # {1, 2, 3, 4, 5}
```

Dictionaries: Key-Value Pairs

Dictionaries store data as key-value pairs. They are incredibly useful for fast data retrieval.

Creating and Using Dictionaries

python

Copy code

```python
my_dict = {"name": "Alice", "age": 25}
print(my_dict["name"])  # Alice
```

Adding and Changing Items: Dictionaries are mutable.

python

Copy code

```python
my_dict["language"] = "Python"
print(my_dict)  # {'name': 'Alice', 'age': 25, 'language': 'Python'}
```

A Practical Example: A Simple Phonebook

Let's create a phonebook using a dictionary to understand how these data structures are used in a real-world context:

python

Copy code

```python
phonebook = {
```

```python
    "Alice": "123-456-7890",
    "Bob": "987-654-3210",
    "Carol": "555-123-4567"
}

# Adding a new entry
phonebook["Dave"] = "555-777-8888"


# Retrieving a number
print(phonebook["Alice"])  # 123-456-7890


# Removing an entry
del phonebook["Bob"]

print(phonebook)          # {'Alice': '123-456-7890', 'Carol': '555-123-4567', 'Dave': '555-777-8888'}
```

Key Learning Points

Lists are mutable sequences, useful for storing an ordered collection of items.

Tuples are immutable sequences, perfect for fixed data sets.

Sets are unordered collections of unique elements, used for operations like unions and intersections.

Dictionaries store data as key-value pairs, ideal for fast lookups.

With a firm grasp of Python's data structures, you can handle a wide range of data management tasks more effectively. These structures are fundamental to Python programming and form the basis of more complex data manipulation and analysis techniques you will encounter as you advance. Experiment with them, and you'll discover their power and versatility in solving real-world problems.

CHAPTER 7: WORKING WITH FILES

Interacting with the File System in Python

One of the most practical skills in any programming language is the ability to read from and write-to files. In this chapter, we'll explore how Python handles file operations, allowing you to store and retrieve data from various file formats.

Basic File Operations: Reading and Writing

Opening a File

The open() function is the key to file manipulation in Python. It requires two main arguments: the file path and the mode (e.g., read, write).

Reading from a File

To read the contents of a file, you open it in 'read' mode ('r') and use the read() method.

```python
Copy code
file = open('example.txt', 'r')
content = file.read()
file.close()
print(content)
```

Always remember to close the file using file.close() to free up system resources.

Writing to a File

Writing to a file is similar, but you open it in 'write' mode ('w'). If the file doesn't exist, Python creates it.

python

Copy code

```
file = open('example.txt', 'w')
file.write('Hello, Python!')
file.close()
```

The with Statement

The with statement simplifies file handling by automatically taking care of closing the file.

python

Copy code

```
with open('example.txt', 'r') as file:
    content = file.read()
    print(content)
```

Handling Different File Formats

Python can work with various file formats. Let's look at how to handle text files, CSV files, and JSON data.

Text Files

You've already seen basic text file operations. They are straightforward and useful for simple data storage.

CSV Files

CSV (Comma-Separated Values) files are commonly used for storing tabular data. Python's csv module makes it easy to read and write CSV files.

python
Copy code
```python
import csv

# Writing to a CSV file
with open('example.csv', 'w', newline='') as file:
    writer = csv.writer(file)
    writer.writerow(["Name", "Age"])
    writer.writerow(["Alice", 30])
    writer.writerow(["Bob", 25])

# Reading from a CSV file
with open('example.csv', 'r') as file:
    reader = csv.reader(file)
    for row in reader:
        print(row)
```

JSON Files

JSON (JavaScript Object Notation) is a popular format for data interchange. Python's json module allows you to read and write JSON data.

python
Copy code
```python
import json
```

```python
# Writing JSON data
data = {"Name": "Alice", "Age": 30}
with open('example.json', 'w') as file:
    json.dump(data, file)

# Reading JSON data
with open('example.json', 'r') as file:
    data = json.load(file)
    print(data)
```

A Practical Example: A Simple Note-Taking App

Let's create a simple note-taking application that writes and reads notes to and from a file.

```python
python
Copy code
def write_note():
    note = input("Enter your note: ")
    with open('notes.txt', 'a') as file:
        file.write(note + "\n")

def read_notes():
    with open('notes.txt', 'r') as file:
        notes = file.readlines()
        for note in notes:
            print(note.strip())

# Example usage
write_note()
```

read_notes()

Key Learning Points

File Operations such as reading and writing are fundamental for data storage and retrieval in Python.

Different File Formats like text, CSV, and JSON can be handled using Python's built-in modules.

The with statement simplifies file handling by managing file opening and closing operations.

Mastering file operations in Python opens up a wide range of possibilities for data manipulation and storage in your programs. From simple text files to more complex formats like CSV and JSON, Python provides powerful tools to interact with the file system efficiently. Experiment with these concepts to enhance your Python applications with file-handling capabilities.

CHAPTER 8: ERROR AND EXCEPTION HANDLING

Navigating and Resolving Python Errors

In programming, errors and exceptions are inevitable, but handling them gracefully is what sets apart robust applications from fragile ones. In this chapter, we dive into understanding and handling errors and exceptions in Python to ensure your programs run smoothly even when faced with unexpected situations.

Understanding Errors in Python

Errors in Python can be broadly classified into two categories: Syntax Errors and Exceptions.

Syntax Errors

Syntax errors occur when Python encounters incorrect syntax (something that breaks the rules of Python grammar).

python

Copy code

```python
print("Hello world"  # Missing closing parenthesis
```

Python will point out the line where the syntax error occurred and indicate the earliest point in the line where the error was detected.

Exceptions

Exceptions are errors detected during execution. They indicate that something went wrong due to an exceptional condition that the program wasn't able to deal with.

python

Copy code

```python
1 / 0  # This will raise a ZeroDivisionError exception
```

The try-except Block: Handling Exceptions

To handle exceptions, Python provides the try-except block, allowing your program to respond to errors differently than its default behavior.

Basic try-except Usage

python

Copy code

```python
try:
    # Code that might raise an exception
    result = 1 / 0
except ZeroDivisionError:
    # Code that runs if the exception occurs
    print("You can't divide by zero!")
```

Handling Multiple Exceptions

You can handle multiple exceptions by including additional except clauses.

python

Copy code

```python
try:
    # Code that might raise multiple exceptions
    my_list = [1, 2, 3]
    print(my_list[3])  # This will raise an IndexError
except ZeroDivisionError:
    print("Divided by zero!")
except IndexError:
    print("Index out of range!")
```

The else and finally Clauses

else: Runs if the try block did not raise an exception.

finally: Always runs, regardless of whether an exception was raised or not.

python

Copy code

```python
try:
    print("No error occurred.")
except Exception:
    print("An exception occurred.")
else:
    print("This executes if there's no exception.")
finally:
    print("This always executes.")
```

Creating Custom Exceptions

Sometimes, you might want to create your own exceptions for specific error conditions in your application.

Defining Custom Exceptions

Custom exceptions are usually derived from Python's built-in

Exception class.

python

Copy code

```python
class MyCustomError(Exception):
    pass

# Raising the custom exception
raise MyCustomError("Something went wrong")
```

A Practical Example: Validating User Input

Let's use exception handling to ensure that user input is valid in a simple program.

python

Copy code

```python
def get_integer_input():
    while True:
        try:
            return int(input("Enter a number: "))
        except ValueError:
            print("That's not an integer! Try again.")

number = get_integer_input()
print("You entered:", number)
```

Key Learning Points

Syntax Errors and Exceptions are different types of errors in Python.

The try-except block is used to handle exceptions and prevent them from crashing your program.

Custom Exceptions can be defined to handle specific error situations uniquely relevant to your application.

Handling errors and exceptions effectively is crucial for building reliable and resilient Python applications. Understanding how to catch and respond to different types of errors allows you to create a smoother user experience and develop programs that can deal with the unexpected gracefully.

CHAPTER 9: OBJECT-ORIENTED PROGRAMMING

Embracing Objects and Classes in Python

Object-Oriented Programming (OOP) is a paradigm that uses "objects" and "classes" to create models based on the real world environment. This chapter will introduce you to the fundamental concepts of OOP in Python, including classes, objects, inheritance, polymorphism, and encapsulation.

Understanding Classes and Objects

Classes: The Blueprints for Objects

A class in Python is like a blueprint for creating objects. It defines a datatype by bundling data and functionalities together.

python

Copy code

```python
class Dog:
    def __init__(self, name, age):
        self.name = name
        self.age = age

    def bark(self):
```

```python
    return "Woof!"
```

Objects: Instances of Classes

Objects are instances of classes. They encapsulate data and functions pertaining to that class.

python

Copy code

```python
my_dog = Dog("Rex", 5)
print(my_dog.bark())  # Woof!
```

Inheritance: Extending Classes

Inheritance allows new classes to inherit the properties and methods from an existing class.

Creating a Subclass

python

Copy code

```python
class Labrador(Dog):
    def __init__(self, name, age, color):
        super().__init__(name, age)
        self.color = color

    def fetch(self):
        return "Fetches the ball!"
```

```python
buddy = Labrador("Buddy", 3, "Golden")
print(buddy.fetch())  # Fetches the ball!
```

Polymorphism: Many Forms

Polymorphism allows different classes to be treated as the same type. It's the ability of different objects to respond, each in its own way, to the same method call.

Polymorphic Behavior

python

Copy code

```python
class Poodle(Dog):
    def bark(self):
        return "Yap!"

def dog_bark(dog):
    print(dog.bark())

dog_bark(my_dog)  # Woof!
dog_bark(Poodle("Coco", 4))  # Yap!
```

Encapsulation: Hiding Information

Encapsulation is the bundling of data and methods that operate on that data. It restricts direct access to some of an object's components, which is a good way to prevent accidental modification.

Using Private Attributes and Methods

python

Copy code

```python
class Cat:
    def __init__(self, name):
        self.__name = name  # Private attribute

    def speak(self):
        return f"Meow! I'm {self.__name}"
```

```python
fluffy = Cat("Fluffy")
print(fluffy.speak())  # Meow! I'm Fluffy
# print(fluffy.__name)  # This will raise an AttributeError
```

A Practical Example: A Simple School System

Let's create a simple class hierarchy to represent a school system.

python
Copy code

```python
class Person:
    def __init__(self, name):
        self.name = name

class Student(Person):
    def study(self):
        return f"{self.name} is studying."

class Teacher(Person):
    def teach(self):
        return f"{self.name} is teaching."

# Creating instances
alice = Student("Alice")
bob = Teacher("Bob")

print(alice.study())  # Alice is studying.
print(bob.teach())   # Bob is teaching.
```

Key Learning Points

Classes and Objects are the core of OOP in Python.

Inheritance allows new classes to extend existing ones.

Polymorphism enables objects of different classes to be treated as objects of a common superclass.

Encapsulation is about bundling data and methods that manipulate that data within a single unit, or class.

Object-Oriented Programming is a powerful paradigm that helps you organize and structure your Python code in a logical and reusable manner. By mastering OOP concepts, you can create more complex, scalable, and maintainable applications. Experiment with these concepts to see how you can apply OOP principles in your Python projects.

CHAPTER 10: ADVANCED PYTHON CONCEPTS

Delving into Python's Powerful Advanced Features

As you grow more comfortable with Python's basics, you're ready to explore some of its more advanced and powerful features. This chapter will introduce you to list comprehensions, generators, decorators, and context managers, tools that can significantly enhance the efficiency and readability of your code.

List Comprehensions: Concise and Elegant

List comprehensions provide a concise way to create lists. They consist of brackets containing an expression followed by a for clause, and optionally, if clauses. They're a more readable and efficient way to create lists.

Basic List Comprehension

python

Copy code

```python
squares = [x**2 for x in range(10)]
print(squares) # [0, 1, 4, 9, 16, 25, 36, 49, 64, 81]
```

Conditional List Comprehension

python

Copy code

```python
even_squares = [x**2 for x in range(10) if x % 2 == 0]
print(even_squares)  # [0, 4, 16, 36, 64]
```

Generators: Efficient Iteration

Generators are a way to create iterators in a very efficient way. They use the yield statement to produce a sequence of values lazily, meaning they generate values one at a time and on the fly, without storing them in memory.

Creating a Generator

python

Copy code

```python
def count_down(num):
    while num > 0:
        yield num
        num -= 1

for i in count_down(5):
    print(i)  # Prints 5, 4, 3, 2, 1
```

Decorators: Modifying Function Behavior

Decorators are a very powerful and useful tool in Python since they allow you to modify the behavior of a function without permanently modifying it.

Basic Decorator

python

Copy code

```python
def my_decorator(func):
```

```python
    def wrapper():
        print("Something is happening before the function is called.")
        func()
        print("Something is happening after the function is called.")
    return wrapper

@my_decorator
def say_hello():
    print("Hello!")

say_hello()
```

Context Managers: Handling Resources

Context managers allow you to allocate and release resources precisely when you want to. The most common way to use them is with the with statement.

Using a Context Manager

python

Copy code

```python
with open('file.txt', 'w') as file:
    file.write('Hello, Python!')
```

This ensures that the file is properly closed after its suite finishes, even if an exception is raised.

A Practical Example: A File Processing Script

Let's create a script that uses these advanced features to read a file, process its contents, and write the output to another file.

python

Copy code

```python
# Using list comprehensions and a context manager to read and process a file
with open('input.txt', 'r') as file:
    lines = [line.strip().upper() for line in file]


# Using a generator to lazily process lines
def process_lines(lines):
    for line in lines:
        yield f"Processed: {line}"


# Writing the processed lines to another file
with open('output.txt', 'w') as file:
    for processed_line in process_lines(lines):
        file.write(processed_line + '\n')
```

Key Learning Points

List Comprehensions offer a more readable and efficient way to create lists.

Generators are used for lazy evaluation, generating values on the fly and reducing memory usage.

Decorators provide a simple syntax for calling higher-order functions.

Context Managers help you manage resources (like file operations) efficiently and safely.

By understanding these advanced Python concepts, you can write more sophisticated and optimized code. These features not only add elegance to your Python scripts but also enhance their performance and scalability. Experiment with them to appreciate the depth and power of Python as a programming language.

CHAPTER 11: INTRODUCTION TO WEB DEVELOPMENT WITH PYTHON

Stepping into the World of Python Web Frameworks

Python is not only a language for scripting and data analysis but also a powerful tool for web development. In this chapter, we'll explore the basics of web development using Python, focusing on popular web frameworks like Flask and Django, and build a simple web application.

Why Python for Web Development?

Python's simplicity, readability, and vast array of libraries make it a great choice for web development. Frameworks like Flask and Django provide the tools to build robust, scalable, and maintainable web applications efficiently.

Flask: Lightweight and Flexible

Flask is a micro web framework. It's lightweight, easy to use, and ideal for small to medium-sized web applications. Flask is also flexible, allowing developers to choose their tools and libraries.

Getting Started with Flask

Installation: To install Flask, simply run pip install flask.

Basic Application:

python
Copy code

```python
from flask import Flask
app = Flask(__name__)

@app.route('/')
def home():
    return 'Hello, Flask!'

if __name__ == '__main__':
    app.run(debug=True)
```

This code creates a basic web server that displays "Hello, Flask!" on the home page.

Django: The Full-Featured Framework

Django is a high-level web framework that encourages rapid development and clean, pragmatic design. It's suitable for larger projects with its "batteries-included" approach.

Basics of Django

Installation: Install Django using pip install django.

Creating a Project:

Run django-admin startproject myproject to create a new project.

Navigate into your project directory and run python manage.py startapp myapp to create a new app within your project.

Basic View:

In myapp/views.py:

python

Copy code

```python
from django.http import HttpResponse

def home(request):
    return HttpResponse("Hello, Django!")
```

Map this view to a URL in myapp/urls.py.

Building a Simple Web Application

Let's create a simple web application using Flask that displays a form and returns the submitted data.

The Application

Application Setup:

python

Copy code

```python
from flask import Flask, render_template, request

app = Flask(__name__)
```

HTML Form:

Create a file templates/form.html:

html

Copy code

```html
<html>
<body>
    <form action="/submit" method="post">
        Name: <input type="text" name="name"><br>
        <input type="submit" value="Submit">
    </form>
</body>
</html>
```

View Functions:

python

Copy code

```python
@app.route('/')
def form():
    return render_template('form.html')


@app.route('/submit', methods=['POST'])
def submit():
    name = request.form['name']
    return f'Hello, {name}!'
```

Running the Application:

Run app.run(debug=True) to start the server. Visit localhost:5000 in your browser to view the form.

Key Learning Points

Flask is a lightweight and flexible framework suitable for small to medium web projects.

Django is a more full-featured framework, great for larger applications with its "batteries-included" approach.

Building a simple web application involves setting up a server, creating view functions, and rendering templates.

Getting started with web development in Python opens a vast field of opportunities. Whether you choose Flask for its simplicity and flexibility or Django for its robustness and efficiency, Python's frameworks offer the tools to build a wide range of web applications, from simple personal projects to large-scale enterprise solutions. Experiment with these frameworks to find which best suits your needs and projects.

CHAPTER 12:
DATA SCIENCE AND MACHINE LEARNING BASICS

Embarking on a Journey with Python into Data Science and AI

Data science and machine learning are rapidly growing fields that offer exciting opportunities to derive meaningful insights from data and build intelligent systems. Python, with its rich ecosystem of libraries, is a cornerstone in these domains. This chapter introduces you to the basics of data science and machine learning using Python, focusing on the NumPy and Pandas libraries, and provides an overview of machine learning.

NumPy: Numerical Python

NumPy is the fundamental package for scientific computing in Python. It provides support for large, multi-dimensional arrays and matrices, along with a collection of mathematical functions to operate on these arrays.

Basic NumPy Operations

Installation: Install NumPy using pip install numpy.

Creating Arrays:

python
Copy code

```python
import numpy as np

a = np.array([1, 2, 3])
print(a)  # Output: [1 2 3]
```

Array Operations:

python
Copy code

```python
b = np.array([[1, 2, 3], [4, 5, 6]])
print(b.shape)  # Output: (2, 3)
print(b + a)    # Output: [[2 4 6] [5 7 9]]
```

Pandas: Data Analysis Made Easy

Pandas is an open-source library providing high-performance, easy-to-use data structures, and data analysis tools. It's particularly suited for data manipulation and analysis.

Getting Started with Pandas

Installation: Install Pandas using pip install pandas.

DataFrames and Series:

Series: A one-dimensional labeled array.

python
Copy code

```python
s = pd.Series([1, 3, 5, np.nan, 6, 8])
print(s)
```

DataFrame: A two-dimensional labeled data structure with columns.

python

Copy code

```python
import pandas as pd

data = {'Name': ['Alice', 'Bob', 'Charlie'],
        'Age': [25, 30, 35],
        'City': ['New York', 'Los Angeles', 'Chicago']}
df = pd.DataFrame(data)
print(df)
```

Basic Data Operations:

Reading data from files, data manipulation, filtering, and aggregation are fundamental operations in Pandas.

Introduction to Machine Learning with Python

Machine learning involves teaching computers to learn from and make predictions or decisions based on data. Python's simplicity and rich library ecosystem make it an ideal language for machine learning.

Key Python Libraries for Machine Learning

Scikit-learn: A powerful tool for machine learning that provides simple and efficient tools for data analysis and mining.

TensorFlow and PyTorch: Libraries for deep learning that provide tools to create complex neural networks.

A Simple Machine Learning Example

Using Scikit-learn to create a simple linear regression model:

python

Copy code

```python
from sklearn.linear_model import LinearRegression
from sklearn.model_selection import train_test_split
import numpy as np

# Sample data
X = np.array([[1, 1], [1, 2], [2, 2], [2, 3]])
y = np.dot(X, np.array([1, 2])) + 3

# Splitting data into training and testing sets
X_train, X_test, y_train, y_test = train_test_split(X, y, test_size=0.2)

# Create a linear regression model
model = LinearRegression().fit(X_train, y_train)

# Make predictions
predictions = model.predict(X_test)
```

Key Learning Points

NumPy is essential for numerical computations in Python.

Pandas simplifies data manipulation and analysis.

Python's ecosystem, including libraries like Scikit-learn, TensorFlow, and PyTorch, makes it a prime choice for machine learning and AI.

This introduction to data science and machine learning with Python is just the tip of the iceberg. As you dive deeper, you'll discover the vast potential of Python in processing, analyzing, and drawing insights from data, as well as its power in building intelligent models that can learn from data and make predictions. This field is vast and constantly evolving, offering endless opportunities for exploration and innovation.

CHAPTER 13: PROJECT - BUILDING A SMALL PYTHON APPLICATION

Applying Python Concepts in a Real-World Scenario

It's time to put your Python skills into practice! This chapter guides you through building a small but functional Python application, integrating various concepts we've learned so far. We'll create a simple command-line tool, a to-do list application, that allows users to add, view, and delete tasks.

Overview of the Project

Our to-do list application will:

Store tasks in a file for persistence.

Allow users to add new tasks.

Display existing tasks.

Delete tasks.

Handle user inputs and potential errors gracefully.

Setting Up the Project

First, create a new Python file named todo_app.py. This file will contain all our application code.

Step 1: Designing the Task Model

We'll start by creating a simple model for our tasks. For simplicity, each task will just be a string.

python

Copy code

```python
tasks = []
```

Step 2: Reading and Writing Tasks to a File

We'll use file handling to persist tasks between application runs.

Writing to a File

python

Copy code

```python
def save_tasks():
    with open("tasks.txt", "w") as file:
        for task in tasks:
            file.write(task + "\n")
```

Reading from a File

python

Copy code

```python
def load_tasks():
    try:
        with open("tasks.txt", "r") as file:
            for line in file:
                tasks.append(line.strip())
    except FileNotFoundError:
        pass  # It's okay if the file doesn't exist yet

load_tasks()
```

Step 3: Adding Tasks

We need a function to add new tasks to our list.

python

Copy code

```python
def add_task(task):
    tasks.append(task)
    save_tasks()
```

Step 4: Viewing Tasks

Displaying tasks is straightforward.

python

Copy code

```python
def view_tasks():
    for index, task in enumerate(tasks, start=1):
        print(f"{index}. {task}")
```

Step 5: Deleting Tasks

Let users delete tasks by specifying the task number.

python

Copy code

```python
def delete_task(task_number):
    if 0 < task_number <= len(tasks):
        del tasks[task_number - 1]
        save_tasks()
    else:
        print("Invalid task number.")
```

Step 6: User Interface

We'll create a simple text-based interface.

python
Copy code

```python
def main():
    while True:
        print("\nTo-Do List")
        print("1. Add a task")
        print("2. View tasks")
        print("3. Delete a task")
        print("4. Exit")

        choice = input("Choose an option: ")

        if choice == "1":
            task = input("Enter a task: ")
            add_task(task)
        elif choice == "2":
            view_tasks()
        elif choice == "3":
            task_number = int(input("Enter task number to delete: "))
            delete_task(task_number)
        elif choice == "4":
            break
        else:
            print("Invalid choice. Please try again.")

if __name__ == "__main__":
```

    main()

Key Learning Points

Integrating Concepts: This project integrates basic Python syntax, functions, file handling, and error management.

Practical Application: By building a real-world application, you get to see how different aspects of Python come together to solve problems.

Incremental Development: Start simple and gradually add more features and complexity. This approach helps in understanding and debugging your code effectively.

Congratulations on building your first Python application! This project serves as a practical example of how you can use Python to solve real-world problems. As you continue to learn and grow as a Python developer, you'll find that the possibilities are truly endless. Keep experimenting, coding, and challenging yourself with new projects!

CHAPTER 14: BEST PRACTICES AND FURTHER RESOURCES

Elevating Your Python Skills and Continuing Your Journey

You've learned a lot about Python, but the journey doesn't end here. This final chapter is dedicated to refining your skills and guiding you toward a future of continuous learning and improvement. We'll cover best practices for writing clean, Pythonic code and provide resources for further education and exploration.

Writing Clean Code

Readability Matters

Python's philosophy emphasizes readability. Clean code is not just about working code, but also about writing code that others (and your future self) can understand.

Use Clear, Descriptive Names: Variable and function names should reflect their purpose.

Keep Functions Short and Focused: Each function should perform one task or aspect of a task.

Avoid Deep Nesting: Too many nested loops or conditions can make your code hard to follow. Try to refactor deeply nested structures.

Pythonic Principles

The Zen of Python

To understand what "Pythonic" means, you can always refer to the Zen of Python by typing import this in the Python console. It's a collection of aphorisms that capture the spirit of Python's design philosophy.

"Beautiful is better than ugly.": Strive for clarity and simplicity in your code.

"Explicit is better than implicit.": Clear code beats clever code. Make your intentions clear.

"There should be one-- and preferably only one --obvious way to do it.": Python encourages using the most straightforward solution to a problem.

Advanced Python Concepts

Continuously improve your skills by exploring advanced Python topics.

Asynchronous Programming: Learn about asyncio for handling asynchronous tasks.

Design Patterns: Familiarize yourself with common design patterns in Python.

Testing: Write tests for your code using frameworks like unittest and pytest.

Further Resources

Online Learning Platforms

Coursera, edX, Udacity: These platforms offer Python courses from basic to advanced levels, including specialized fields like data science and machine learning.

Codecademy, LeetCode, HackerRank: Practice your coding skills and solve challenges in Python.

Books

"Fluent Python" by Luciano Ramalho: A great read for understanding Python's features and best practices.

"Effective Python" by Brett Slatkin: Learn more about writing idiomatic Python code.

"Python Crash Course" by Eric Matthes: A hands-on, project-based introduction to Python.

Communities

Stack Overflow: Great for getting answers to specific questions and engaging with other developers.

GitHub: Contribute to open-source Python projects to gain real-world coding experience.

Reddit, Python.org Forums: Join discussions and stay updated with the Python community.

Conclusion

Remember, learning to code is a journey, not a destination. The more you code, the better you will become. Stay curious, keep exploring new ideas, and don't be afraid to build something from scratch. Python is a tool that empowers you to bring your ideas to life, so use it, explore it, and most importantly, enjoy it!

You are now equipped with the knowledge, best practices, and resources to further your Python journey. This is just the beginning of a rewarding path in programming. Embrace the challenges ahead, and keep coding!

We are adding a **bonus tutorial** on HTML and CSS, especially considering how often these technologies are used alongside

Python in web development.

1. INTRODUCTION TO WEB DEVELOPMENT

Welcome to the world of web development, an exciting and ever-evolving field that combines creativity and technical skills to create and maintain websites. This chapter will introduce you to the foundational elements of web development: HTML, CSS, and JavaScript. We'll also explore how web browsers render these technologies to display web pages.

Understanding the Role of HTML, CSS, and JavaScript in Web Development

Web development primarily involves three core technologies, each with its unique role:

HTML: The Skeleton of the Web

HTML (HyperText Markup Language) is the standard markup language used to create the structure of web pages.

Think of HTML as the skeleton of a website, providing the basic structure and content.

HTML uses tags to denote different elements such as headings, paragraphs, links, images, and more.

CSS: The Stylist of the Web

CSS (Cascading Style Sheets) is the language used to style HTML documents.

CSS determines how HTML elements should be displayed,

controlling layout, colors, fonts, and even some animations.

Imagine CSS as the clothing and makeup that style the HTML skeleton, defining the look and feel of the website.

JavaScript: The Brain of the Web

JavaScript is a scripting language that enables interactive features on web pages.

While HTML and CSS are more about structure and style, JavaScript is about behavior.

JavaScript can update content dynamically, handle form submissions, create interactive maps, animations, and much more.

Together, these three technologies create the rich and interactive web experiences we are familiar with today.

The Basics of Web Browsers and How They Render Web Pages

Web browsers are software applications that retrieve, present, and traverse information on the World Wide Web. The most popular browsers include Google Chrome, Mozilla Firefox, Safari, and Microsoft Edge.

How Browsers Render Web Pages

Fetching Resources: The browser fetches the HTML, CSS, and JavaScript files from the web server. This is done through HTTP (Hypertext Transfer Protocol).

Parsing HTML: The browser parses the HTML file to understand the structure and content of the web page. This process creates a DOM (Document Object Model) tree.

Rendering Process:

CSS Styling: The browser applies CSS to the HTML structure. The styling information is combined with the DOM tree to create a 'render tree' that knows how each node should be displayed.

JavaScript Interaction: JavaScript is then executed, which may manipulate the DOM and alter the final page.

Layout and Painting: The browser calculates the exact position and size of each element (layout), and then it 'paints' the content on the screen.

Reflow and Repaint: If a script or user interaction changes the DOM or CSS, the browser may reflow (recalculate layout) and repaint the page.

Understanding this process is key to becoming an effective web developer. It helps in optimizing web pages for speed, efficiency, and responsiveness across different browsers and devices.

This introduction sets the stage for your journey into the intricate world of web development. By understanding the roles of HTML, CSS, and JavaScript, and how browsers bring them together, you are now ready to dive deeper into each technology and start building your own web pages.

2. GETTING STARTED WITH HTML

Welcome to the foundational building block of web development: HTML. In this chapter, we'll explore the basic structure of a web page, the essentials of HTML syntax, and create your very first HTML page. Let's dive into the world of tags, elements, and attributes!

Introduction to HTML: Structure of a Web Page

HTML is used to structure content on the web. A typical web page has a clear structure, defined using various HTML elements:

<!DOCTYPE html>: This declaration defines the document type and version of HTML.

<html>: The root element that wraps the entire content.

<head>: Contains meta-information about the document like its title, character set, and links to CSS files.

<body>: Houses the content of the web page, such as text, images, links, etc.

HTML Basics: Elements, Tags, and Attributes

Elements and Tags

An HTML element typically consists of a start tag and an end tag, with content in between:

html

Copy code

```
<p>This is a paragraph.</p>
```

In this example, <p> is the start tag, and </p> is the end tag. The element in this case is the entire structure, including the tags and the content.

Attributes

Attributes provide additional information about elements. They are defined within the start tag:

html

Copy code

```
<a href="https://www.example.com">Visit Example.com</a>
```

Here, href is an attribute of the <a> (anchor) element, specifying the link's destination.

Creating Your First HTML Page: "Hello, World!"

Let's create a simple HTML file:

Open a text editor (like Notepad or TextEdit).

Type the following HTML code:

html

Copy code

```
<!DOCTYPE html>
<html>
    <head>
```

```html
    <title>My First Page</title>
  </head>
  <body>
    <h1>Hello, World!</h1>
  </body>
</html>
```

Save the file with a .html extension, for example, hello.html.

Open the file in a web browser to see your first HTML page.

Key HTML Elements: Paragraphs, Headings, Lists, and Links

Paragraphs and Headings

Paragraphs (<p>): Used to define a block of text.

Headings (<h1> to <h6>): Used to define headings, with <h1> being the highest level.

Lists

Unordered Lists (<ul>): For a bulleted list.

Ordered Lists (<ol>): For a numbered list.

List Items (<li>): Define items in a list.

Links

Anchor (<a>): Used to define hyperlinks.

Adding Images and Multimedia

To add images, use the <img> tag:

html

Copy code

```html
<img src="image.jpg" alt="Description of the image">
```

src specifies the path to the image, and alt provides alternative text.

Understanding the Document Object Model (DOM)

The DOM is a programming interface for web documents.

It represents the page so that programs can change the document structure, style, and content.

The DOM represents the document as nodes and objects; thus, programming languages can interact with the page.

By grasping these fundamental concepts of HTML, you've taken the first step into web development. HTML is the cornerstone of all web design, and understanding it deeply will aid in your journey as you start to explore more complex web development concepts.

3. DIVING DEEPER INTO HTML

After covering the basics of HTML, it's time to delve deeper into some of its more intricate aspects. In this chapter, we'll explore how to create tables, build forms, understand the importance of semantic HTML, and consider accessibility in web design. These concepts are crucial for creating well-structured, user-friendly, and accessible web pages.

Creating Tables

Tables in HTML are used to display data in a tabular format. A basic table is created using the <table>, <tr>, <th>, and <td> tags.

<table>: Defines the table.

<tr>: Table row.

<th>: Table header.

<td>: Table cell.

html

Copy code

```
<table>
  <tr>
    <th>Name</th>
    <th>Email</th>
  </tr>
```

```
<tr>
  <td>Alice</td>
  <td>alice@example.com</td>
</tr>
<tr>
  <td>Bob</td>
  <td>bob@example.com</td>
</tr>
</table>
```

Forms and Input Elements: Building a Basic Contact Form

Forms are used to collect user input. A basic form includes various input elements like text fields, radio buttons, checkboxes, and buttons.

Structure of a Form

<form>: The container for the form elements.

<input>: For user input.

<label>: Provides a label for form elements.

<textarea>: For multi-line text input.

<button>: A clickable button.

Example: A Basic Contact Form

html

Copy code

```
<form action="/submit-form" method="post">
  <label for="name">Name:</label><br>
  <input type="text" id="name" name="name"><br>
  <label for="email">Email:</label><br>
  <input type="email" id="email" name="email"><br>
```

```
<label for="message">Message:</label><br>
<textarea id="message" name="message"></textarea><br>
<button type="submit">Submit</button>
</form>
```

Semantic HTML: Why It Matters

Semantic HTML involves using HTML tags to convey the meaning and structure of your content, not just its appearance. This practice improves readability, SEO, and accessibility.

Examples of Semantic Elements: <article>, <section>, <nav>, <header>, <footer>, <aside>.

Benefits: Helps search engines understand the content, aids screen readers, and improves site navigation.

Accessibility in Web Design

Accessibility in web design means making your website usable for as many people as possible, including those with disabilities.

Alt Text for Images: Describe images with the alt attribute so screen readers can interpret them.

Keyboard Navigation: Ensure your website can be navigated using a keyboard.

Contrast and Color: Use high contrast and avoid color combinations that are hard for colorblind users to differentiate.

Use ARIA Roles: Accessible Rich Internet Applications (ARIA) roles provide additional context to assistive technologies.

html

Copy code

```
<img src="dog.jpg" alt="A friendly dog">
```

By mastering these aspects of HTML, you enhance both the functionality and the accessibility of your web pages. Remember, good web design is not just about how a website looks, but also about how it operates and accommodates all users. This inclusive approach is a cornerstone of modern web development.

4. INTRODUCTION TO CSS

Cascading Style Sheets (CSS) is a powerful tool that works alongside HTML to enhance the visual presentation of web pages. In this chapter, we'll explore the fundamentals of CSS, including its different types, syntax, and some basic styling concepts like the box model. CSS is what takes your web page from a plain document to a visually engaging piece of art.

What is CSS: The Language for Styling Web Pages

CSS is used to control the layout and appearance of HTML elements on a web page. It allows you to apply styles to elements, such as colors, fonts, spacing, and positioning, without altering the HTML structure.

Inline, Internal, and External CSS: When to Use Each

Inline CSS

Defined directly within an HTML element using the style attribute.

Useful for quick, single-element styling, but not efficient for styling multiple elements.

html

Copy code

```
<p style="color: blue;">This is a blue paragraph.</p>
```

Internal CSS

Placed within the <head> section of an HTML document using the <style> tag.

Good for single-page styles, but not efficient for multiple pages.

html

Copy code

```
<style>
  p { color: red; }
</style>
```

External CSS

Defined in separate .css files.

The most efficient method for styling large websites. Styles can be reused across multiple pages.

html

Copy code

```
<link rel="stylesheet" type="text/css" href="styles.css">
```

CSS Syntax: Selectors, Properties, and Values

Basic Syntax

Selectors: Specify the HTML elements to be styled.

Properties: Define what to style within the elements.

Values: Determine how the properties will be styled.

css

Copy code

```
selector {
  property: value;
}
```

For example:

css

Copy code

```
p {
  color: green;
  font-size: 14px;
}
```

Basic Styling: Colors, Fonts, and Sizes

Colors

Can be specified by name, HEX, RGB, or HSL values.

css

Copy code

```
h1 { color: #ff4500; } /* orange color */
```

Fonts

Define the typeface of your text.

css

Copy code

```
body { font-family: Arial, sans-serif; }
```

Sizes

Specify the size of various elements like text, boxes, etc.

css

Copy code

p { font-size: 16px; }

The Box Model: Margins, Borders, Padding, and Content

Every element in CSS is made up of a box, and understanding this box model is crucial for layout control.

Content: The actual content like text or images.

Padding: Space between the content and the border.

Border: Surrounds the padding and content.

Margin: Space outside the border, separating the element from others.

css

Copy code

```
.box {
  width: 300px;
  padding: 10px;
  border: 5px solid gray;
  margin: 20px;
}
```

Understanding and applying CSS effectively can drastically improve the user experience of your web pages. It's a critical skill for creating responsive, accessible, and visually appealing websites. As you continue to explore CSS, you'll find it a versatile and essential tool in your web development arsenal.

5. ADVANCED CSS TECHNIQUES

As you become more comfortable with the basics of CSS, it's time to explore some advanced techniques that can bring sophistication and interactivity to your web designs. This chapter delves into modern layout methods like Flexbox and Grid, responsive design principles, enhancing lists and navigation bars, utilizing pseudo-classes for interactive effects, and adding flair with transitions and animations.

Layout Techniques: Flexbox and Grid Systems

Flexbox

Flexbox is a layout model that allows you to design complex layouts with ease. It's ideal for one-dimensional layouts (either in a row or a column).

Use Flexbox for aligning items, distributing space, and creating flexible layouts.

css

Copy code

```
.container {
  display: flex;
  justify-content: space-between;
}
```

Grid

Grid Layout is a two-dimensional layout system. It's powerful for creating complex web layouts on both rows and columns.

Use Grid to design layouts with multiple rows and columns, and to align content within.

css

Copy code

```css
.grid-container {
  display: grid;
  grid-template-columns: auto auto auto;
}
```

Responsive Design and Media Queries

Responsive Design ensures that your web page looks good on all devices (desktops, tablets, and phones).

Media Queries are a key tool in responsive design, allowing you to apply CSS styles depending on the device's characteristics, like its width, height, or orientation.

css

Copy code

```css
@media screen and (max-width: 600px) {
  .container {
    flex-direction: column;
  }
}
```

Styling Lists and Navigation Bars

Use CSS to transform lists into visually appealing navigation bars.

Style <ul>, <li>, and <a> elements to create horizontal or vertical navigation menus.

css

Copy code

```css
nav ul {
  list-style-type: none;
  margin: 0;
  padding: 0;
  overflow: hidden;
  background-color: #333333;
}

nav li {
  float: left;
}

nav li a {
  display: block;
  color: white;
  text-align: center;
  padding: 14px 16px;
  text-decoration: none;
}
```

Hover, Focus, and Other Pseudo-Classes

Pseudo-classes like :hover, :focus, and :active add interactive states to your elements.

:hover is commonly used to change the style of an element when it's hovered over by a mouse.

css

Copy code

```css
button:hover {
  background-color: blue;
}
```

Transitions and Animations

Transitions

CSS Transitions smoothly change a property over a given duration.

They enhance user experience by providing visual feedback.

css

Copy code

```css
.transition {
  transition: background-color 0.5s ease;
}
```

Animations

CSS Animations allow more control over the intermediate steps of a CSS property transition.

Use @keyframes to define the animation and apply it to elements.

css

Copy code

```css
@keyframes example {
  from {background-color: red;}
  to {background-color: yellow;}
}

.animation {
  animation-name: example;
  animation-duration: 4s;
}
```

These advanced CSS techniques are essential for creating modern, professional, and responsive web designs. As you practice these concepts, you'll develop a stronger grasp of how to control layouts, create interactive elements, and build visually dynamic web pages.

6. INTEGRATING HTML AND CSS

This chapter is dedicated to the art of seamlessly integrating HTML and CSS, the core technologies behind web layout and design. Here, we'll delve into creating simple yet effective web page layouts, adopt best practices for structuring your HTML and CSS, ensure your website's compatibility across various browsers, and explore effective debugging and troubleshooting strategies.

Building a Simple Web Page Layout

Structuring with HTML

Foundation with HTML: Begin by crafting the structure of your web content using HTML. Implement semantic elements such as <header>, <nav>, <main>, and <footer> to enhance readability and search engine optimization (SEO).

Example Layout:

html

Copy code

```
<header>...</header>
<nav>...</nav>
<main>...</main>
<footer>...</footer>
```

Styling with CSS

Enhancing Style with CSS: Once the HTML structure is in place, use CSS to bring style to your elements. This involves setting properties like widths, heights, colors, fonts, and positioning to define the look and feel of your web page.

Best Practices for Structuring HTML and CSS

Organize Your Files

Separation of Concerns: Keep your CSS separate from your HTML. Employ external stylesheets for streamlined maintenance and enhanced performance.

Consistent Naming Conventions

Clear Identifiers: Utilize descriptive and clear class and ID names in both HTML and CSS. This promotes easier readability and efficient maintenance.

Mobile-First Approach

Responsive Design: Begin your design with mobile devices in mind, and then scale up to larger screens using CSS media queries.

Cross-Browser Compatibility and Testing

Use Reset CSS

Uniformity Across Browsers: Apply a CSS reset to ensure consistent styling across different web browsers.

Vendor Prefixes

Browser-Specific Styles: Use vendor prefixes like -webkit- (Chrome, Safari), -moz- (Firefox), and -ms- (Internet Explorer) to ensure cross-browser compatibility.

Regular Testing

Utilize Tools for Testing: Leverage browser developer tools and platforms like BrowserStack to test your website across various browsers and devices.

Debugging and Troubleshooting

Web Developer Tools

Real-Time Inspection and Modification: Use browser developer tools for inspecting elements, tweaking CSS, and real-time debugging.

Validation Tools

Ensure Code Standards: Utilize W3C's HTML and CSS validation services to detect and rectify errors in your code.

By mastering the integration of HTML and CSS, you're well-equipped to create web layouts that are both aesthetically pleasing and functionally robust. Keep these practices in mind as you continue to develop and refine your web development skills.

7. NEXT STEPS IN WEB DEVELOPMENT

Having built a strong foundation in HTML and CSS, you are now poised to take the next steps in your web development journey. This chapter will introduce you to JavaScript, explore modern web development frameworks, and provide resources for further learning and practice.

Introduction to JavaScript and Dynamic Web Pages

JavaScript is the scripting language that enables dynamic interactions on web pages. It's a critical component of modern web development.

JavaScript Basics

Learn the Syntax: Familiarize yourself with JavaScript syntax and fundamental concepts, which are essential for adding interactivity to web pages.

Key Concepts: Variables, functions, loops, and conditional statements.

Manipulating the DOM

Interact with HTML/CSS: Use JavaScript to dynamically manipulate the Document Object Model (DOM), allowing you to modify HTML and CSS on the fly.

Dynamic Content: Add, remove, and modify elements in your web pages in response to user actions.

Event Handling

User Interactions: Implement event handling to make your web pages interactive. This includes responding to user actions like mouse clicks, keyboard input, and touch gestures.

Overview of Modern Web Development Frameworks

The landscape of web development is continuously evolving, with various frameworks and technologies emerging to enhance efficiency and capability.

Front-End Frameworks

React, Vue.js, Angular: These popular JavaScript frameworks offer robust structures for building interactive and efficient front-end web applications.

Component-Based Architecture: Learn how these frameworks utilize reusable components for efficient web development.

Back-End Development

Node.js, Django, Ruby on Rails: Dive into the world of server-side programming. These technologies are used to build the back-end of web applications, handling database interactions, server logic, and application integration.

Full-Stack Development: Understanding both front-end and back-end technologies makes you a versatile developer, capable of handling comprehensive web projects.

Resources for Further Learning and Practice

Online Courses

Comprehensive Learning Platforms: Platforms like Coursera, Udemy, and freeCodeCamp offer structured and in-depth courses that cover various aspects of web development, from beginner to advanced levels.

Documentation and Tutorials

Reliable References: Utilize MDN Web Docs and W3Schools for up-to-date tutorials, documentation, and best practices in web development.

Community and Forums

Join Developer Communities: Engage with developer communities on Stack Overflow, GitHub, and Reddit. These platforms offer invaluable resources for support, collaboration, and staying updated with industry trends.

Your journey in web development is one of continuous learning and adaptation. By expanding your skills into JavaScript and various web development frameworks, and tapping into the wealth of resources and communities available, you're well on your way to becoming a proficient and versatile web developer. Keep exploring, building, and refining your skills – the world of web development awaits!

Thank you for your purchase of "Coding with Python: From First Steps to Advanced Mastery".

I sincerely hope this turorial helps you on your coding journey. Happy Coding!